This book is dedicated to, the loved ones I lost.

When we lose someone, we love, we must learn not to live without them but to live with the memories, lessons, and love they left behind.

Acknowledgments

To my parents, Joe & Nancy, thank you for always seeing the potential
in me even when I couldn't see it in myself. For the countless days and nights of encouragement that I didn't know I needed until now. The push you gave me during my early childhood allotted me the space for the creativity that I now possess. I'm beyond grateful for the life lessons you taught me that have now landed me here. I love, miss, & appreciate you both so much.

To my brother, Brandon, you always had my back and never held back your input. Your blunt and direct approach always put things in the right perspective for me. There was so much we had to accomplish, and I vow to continue to strive to complete the goal. I love & miss you bro.

To my brother in love, Kyle. So full of life and energy. Always eager to tell me how dope I was and to keep grinding because the world needed to hear me. I live in your vibe and energy. It keeps me going even when I want to give up. Your words "This that Fly" will always live in my head. I love and miss you, kid!

My mother in Love, Mommy. Your love never showed any doubt. It always operated as if you birthed me yourself. Your stern but loving support was EVERYTHING I never knew I needed. I thank you for never holding back and loving me unconditionally. I love you and miss you!

To my children, everything I do is for y'all. I will always strive to be better and provide a better lifestyle for all of you. My goal is that you all can someday say that's my dad with your head held high with pride and confidence. I do and will always love you all unconditionally.

And finally, My Wife. You're my number 1 supporter. Thank you for always seeing my vision and believing in it. For always helping me navigate it the right way and allowing me the time and space to complete the course. Thank you for never letting me give up and pushing me to finish the race. A man is only as strong as the woman that holds him up… Thank you for holding me up, Beautiful. I love you!

Damn Randy

My Stories

1. I know Santa

2. In Too Deep

3. Freshman Friday

4. Red Iversons

5. I've Fallen and I Can't Get Up

6. Chicken Wing

7. Mr. Funkledick

8. G.E.D.

9. The Bushes

10. Where's My Money

11. Monopoly

12. Long Island

13. Dusse

14. BBQ on Edgewood

15. You Going to Jail

I KNOW SANTA

It's Christmas Eve in 1990. As I sit here and impatiently wait for night to arrive, I can't help but hope that I get everything that I asked Santa for. On my list was a drum set, a bike, and a game system. Although I was only 3 and didn't know much about games, I couldn't help but want what everyone else talked about. I was always a spoiled little kid. Didn't see much of my mother but she definitely had the bag or at least that's what I thought. It didn't matter to me much though, what she lacked, my Mima made up for. That's what I called my grandmother back then, perfection in my eyes! She could do no wrong… Who am I lying to?

I was always mad at her for beating me when I acted out but, spare the rod, spoil the child. She didn't spare the rod most time, but I was spoiled as hell, and I knew she loved me. None of my disciplinary ass whippings were out of hate, instead the total opposite. She loved me so much and wanted

7

me to be prepared for what I would go
through later in life.

"Watch out for sneaky people" is what
she would say.

"Don't trust people who talk about
their friends, because they'll talk about you
too."

I can still hear her to this day. A lot of what
she said still sticks with me and applies
more now than ever. But back to my gifts.

Christmas is here and I'm the 1st one
up.

"WAKE UP, WAKE UP" I'm running
through the house screaming.

I've made my way from the basement, past
the kitchen and here I am in the living room
and there goes my uncle, guess I wasn't the
first one up. Me and my uncle Rome are
close, almost like brothers. He's only 3

years older than me, so we did everything together. He became a barrier for me down the line, almost like a protector but we'll get there.

"Look, Look" he shouted, "We got bikes!"

He's already on the blue one and pointing, suggesting that I get on the red one. As he acts like he's already speeding through the NY streets, my mother enters the living room. Ok so let me explain. There were 11 ppl living in the house and yes, we're all family, or so I thought. There's my Grandparents, the best ppl to ever have walked the face of this earth. Their 8 kids and myself. I know what you're thinking, your grandparents were busy. I thought the same thing but my grandparents fostered children. They had these children from the time my uncle Rome was 3 months old. They were one of us until they weren't. But back to the bikes, so we're chillen when my mother enters and says,

"Rome, you're on the wrong bike."

Rome & I were bothered, wondering how he could be on the wrong bikes and how my mother would know that. The only way would be if she said Santa left the bikes out.

"But I asked for the blue bike," Rome said.

Now my uncle Rome, just like me, was very spoiled. We both got whatever we asked for and up until the day I was born Rome was my mother's baby. He was her youngest brother and a reason for her to spend money. When I arrived, we had to share that coin. As much as Rome loved me, he hated the fact that he had to share my mother. For 3yrs he was the one getting attention and now here I was. This moment became one of those times when my mother responded with

"No, you asked for a Red bike along with that GI Joe."

For Rome, it sent him into one of his fits. He was upset once again, feeling like I always got what I wanted even though I had never said anything. I was cool with having the red bike, Red was my favorite color… EVEN NOW!

While Rome was upset and hurt, I had just discovered that there was no Santa. My uncle was the tough one, always filled with anger even as a child but me… I paid attention to the clues, so I knew how I to move forward. I knew that Rome and I had written letters to Santa, put them in envelopes with a stamp on them, and sealed them. So, the only way for my mother to know what was on Rome's list was for her to have opened it. BOOM! Just like that, I knew there was no Santa. My mother was Santa and moving forward every year after that I just watched her and found more and more evidence to support my theory. It got so bad that to prove my point to Rome I would make mention of something that I wanted last minute and know that it would be under the tree. Time and time again, he doubted me until finally, he could no longer deny what he was seeing but we continued to play the game. We had to pretend that there was a Santa, or we wouldn't get gifts. So, every year we made cookies, wrote letters, and pretended to be asleep while my mother and my grandmother put out gifts acting as if Santa had left them, but this would change me forever.

This was the first act of deceit I was made aware of, and it only got worse,
Stay Tuned!

In Too Deep

Let's fast forward to the summer of 1999. This is the year everything came into perspective for me. Just graduated from elementary school & I'm on my way to JHS 231. This was the cool school because I.S. 59 middle school had to wear uniforms. I couldn't do that. I had established my fashion by now, but before we even get to this the summer is here and I'm enjoying it. I had my crew from Elementary that I hung with all the time and my uncle Rome and his friends… that I was always with when I wasn't with my friends. All older guys and gang members. So, I was able to keep my childhood by hanging with my friends but grew up mentally through my uncle's experiences. See my uncle Rome had started getting in trouble when one of his brothers and his sister told him that he wasn't biologically my Mima's son. He started to feel like he didn't belong, so he went and started doing dumb shit. One of those dumb things was joining a gang. First, it was the neighborhood gang, Farmers Family. Then it was the gangs we found out about at school like LB, which stands for Lost Boys. Ultimately, He became a blood and got so good at it that he climbed the ranks pretty quickly. Hence, he was 15 hanging out with grown ass 25 and 30 year olds. He always said.

"Randy, stay focused and in them books man…"
"Stay out the streets, man"

And of course, I said OK, but I liked the attention he got from it and would eventually want that same attention. But that wasn't the only reason I would take to the streets.

See I never knew my father, I only heard the rumors…
The stories of how crazy he was. Snuggles is what they called him. How could a man

named Snuggles be so tough? All the stories of who he was only made me wanna be like him more without knowing who he really was. He too would become a FRUAD in my eyes. So, it's 1999, summer is almost over, and it's about time to go back to school. But before we go back, I wanted to do one last thing. There was this movie premiering titled In Too Deep starring LL Cool J and Omar Epps. I saw the trailer and immediately knew I had to see this, but I couldn't get anyone to take me. How could I explain to any adult that I wanted to see this rated-R movie about Violence and expect them to understand… They wouldn't! But my aunt… My aunt Elizabeth, my favorite aunt. She never treated me like a child and although there was a 14 year difference we were also like brother and sister. She was the reason I hated white ppl until I was 18 years old. She made me watch Black Panther Party and Malcolm X as a child and ended up marrying a white man

SMH. She was also the reason I found my first love, music. I saw her play the drums when I was young and wanted to do nothing more. She was the first person to put me on the drums and encourage me to sing. I never thought I'd see the day our relationship would end but again, you never know people until you do. At the time, my aunt had this boyfriend who was really into her, he'd do anything for her. He was actively studying to be a detective and wanted to go see the movie In Too Deep as well, and just like that, we were in the movie theater eating candy and drinking slushies. GOD and his Angels from Newark, New Jersey… I still remember that scene as an 11yr old boy. Dude was under the covers tongue fucking the shit out of his girl, and in comes these niggas. He cuts the dude's tongue out and tells her to finish the job herself. I was stuck. That was the most gangster shit I had ever seen in my life but that wasn't what stuck out to me the most.

"You ain't no cop J Reid, You ain't no cop J Reid"

rung in my head for months after watching that movie. He went in a cop and left out a confused and disloyal friend. A lot of people said he was just doing his job, but I definitely didn't see it that way. This man let you in around his family, his kids, gave you the plug to the money and you turned on him?

"But what was he to do" a lot of ppl said. If you asked me, Stop being a cop. Be loyal to who's loyal to you. That changed my perspective on a lot of things moving forward. I don't know if that was for the good or for the bad, but it happened. The next week I turned 12 and was in JHS. And that's when it started.

Stay Tuned!

Freshman Friday

It's the first week of school. I had my clothes laid out from the night before. Khaki pants, a black polo, and my black and red Jordan 14, I was super hyped. My Mima had given me the money to get my sneakers as a birthday present and I didn't wear them until the first day of school. Now I was about to pop out. I was ready to put that shit on and stunt. I wake up, wash my face, brush my teeth, get dressed, and head out the door. Oh, wait, I need money for the bus. My mother had only given me a $20 bill for food and drinks, but I needed change. No worries my uncle Rome said he had me. By this time my uncle Rome walked around with stacks of cash in his pockets. I never knew where he got it from, and I never cared. He made sure I was good and vice versa.

"Come on Ran, I got you," he said.

We head to the Bus and before we even get on one of his homeboys pulls up.

"Y'all need a ride?"

My uncle Rome was all about stunting and although it wasn't a Benz or a BMW, we were still going to pull up bumping music like the cool kids. My uncle Rome went to Springfield High School which was right across the bridge from 231 but he was never there. I knew this because most of the time he was there to get me after school. Like I said, he always had my back.

Day 1 is real chill. I got my old friends with me from Elementary and some new and I'm vibing. I got my Full Ride Bus Pass and I'm good. The next day, the same thing. It's a vibe. I'm loving this. No sitting in one classroom all day, I'm experiencing different personalities from teachers, and the freedom of being able to cut school if I wanted to, just made me feel so alive. And then it happened...

"Freshman Friday, Freshman Friday"

I heard someone scream out and I watched all the 7 graders around me cringe with fear, I was so confused. I had never heard anything about freshman Friday. Was this a boring seminar in the auditorium, or did we have to come back with our parents? I know they weren't about to do a 3-day evaluation. Then I heard someone say,

"I'm not coming to school tomorrow." That made me even more curious.

"Yooo, what's freshman Friday?" I asked.

One of the boys responded,
"That's when the 8th graders pick on and beat up the 7th graders."

Who was going to do what and when? Hell Nah. They had the wrong person. I wasn't nowhere near tough at this moment in my life, but my Uncle Rome was, and he was right across the bridge.

"Ain't nobody gone touch me." I started saying out loud to assert my dominance.

"I'm good" I added before someone's rebuttal asked me.
"Who told you that?"
"I did" I responded.
"Ok, we'll see," the boy said before turning and tapping one of his boys and laughing.

Clearly, he was an 8th grader. He wasn't big in physical stature, but his presence was bigger than the biggest guys around him. I chuckled knowing that when I got home and told my uncle Rome that he was going to be made an example of. I get home, take off my book bag, find something to eat, and turn on the television just like I would any other day. It was now 3:15, Uncle Rome usually didn't come in the house until 4:15 or 4:30 and always gave my Mima some lame excuse about being part of some club at school. She knew damn well he wasn't there but didn't have the energy to follow up with him every time. 4:15 came and I started watching the door but still not worried. But once I locked in on some old reruns of Martin, that my Aunt Elizabeth had recorded on a VHS, and looked up and noticed that it was 6 pm I started to worry a little bit. Not so much about the freshman Friday but more so my uncle. I knew he was out there involved in activities that could potentially get him in trouble and if that didn't, coming home at 6 pm on a school night without permission would.

"Mima, Where's Rome," I asked.
"I was just about to ask you that" she replied.

DAMN, my Uncle Rome was definitely in trouble. He was always the type to be like you, can't get in more trouble, either you're in trouble or you're not. Fucking Dummy was always in extreme trouble. There was never a dull moment, but I say all of that to say Uncle Rome never came home that night. Now I was more worried about him than I was about these bullies, at least until the next morning came and it was time to go to school. Damn… Think Randy! I couldn't come up with shit that would make my grandmother allow me to stay home from school, especially not no fight.

"We don't run from fights and it ain't no fair fights." is what she always told both me and Rome.

Meaning if one fights, so does the other. We stand on those principles to this day. So here we go, today I decided to walk to school.

Me & Law, my best friend, decided to walk and figure out our next move. Law was like me, fresh and fly. Probably a little more flyer. His parents gave him any and everything. He was me on steroids when it came down to being spoiled. We ultimately became family. It went as far as our mothers lying to the teachers and telling them that we were related. Law like me had an Uncle Rome character in his life, it was his brother Racks. Racks & Rome were good friends as well and if Racks saw anyone fucking with me, he was going to deal with it. But Law was one person throughout it all, always had my back! Here we are, we've arrived at school. As we nervously waited for whatever the day was going to bring, surprisingly it brought nothing. 1st period went by, then 2nd. By the time I realized nothing was going on the day was over. Walked outside, greeted my homeboys, and was off to head home to see what was up with my uncle. I was hoping someone had heard something from or about him by now. The smart thing to do would've been to ride the bus but nah we were feeling ourselves. After all the threats we made it through the day, and no one had to get physical. So, me and Law have been walking for 20mins now, discussing which girls have the most potential. We're literally in our neighborhood, maybe 7 minutes from my house at the pace that we're walking at I hear,

"What's up, freshmen?"

FUCK!! I knew it was too good to be true and out of all days there's no one around. We looked over our shoulders to see who said it but didn't recognize these dudes. Who would be dumb enough to challenge us in our neighborhood? We weren't tough but the hood knew us as the little dudes. They were going to take care of us if anyone came outside. Then the little one ran up on me and started to push me around. As he did so I noticed that he had a high school badge on. I wasn't a fighter but after getting pushed around so much I was ready to go. I could feel myself getting worked up and felt the tears sweeping up in my eyes and right as the crowd started to build and that tear fell from my eye I heard,

"Why you fucking with my little cousin."

It was Black, another one of my play cousins from the neighborhood. Black was 6'3 at the time and had an athletic build from playing basketball. He was also a blood but not the same as my Uncle Rome. He respected my uncle Rome, which meant protecting me when Rome wasn't around.

"I'm sorry, we didn't know" is what I started hearing the 2 boys utter.

Now I stood at 5'1 at the time. I was damn near a midget and the little one was maybe 3 inches bigger than me. But the big one, he was damn near the same height as Black. The fear they both had in their eyes was as if they had known they had fucked up. I knew Black was about to annihilate these dudes, but he never got the chance because the next thing I heard was,

"There goes his uncle right there…"

Oh, Shit, My Uncle was walking down the block with 12 of the grimiest and evil men you could ever imagine. They all had looks of who could do the worst thing to you. It would've been terrifying if I didn't know they were on my side. uncle Rome walks up very casually and peaced Black.

"What's the word" he said.

Black started to fill him in that he caught the guys fucking with me and that they were about to jump me. The little guy went to reply,

"No, we were just", when my uncle signaled for him to be quiet.

Now we're in the middle of Thurston with at least 80 ppl surrounding us.

"Randy, these niggas tried to jump you," he asked.
"Yea Unc" I replied.
His funny grin immediately turned rabid.
"Smack Him," he said.

I was so stuck I just looked at him and said "Huh."

This wasn't something we had practiced. He didn't say fuck him up or beat his ass and I can tell that he meant for me to degrade him by slapping him.

"Smack Him," he said again.

I smacked dude and the next thing I saw verified that my uncle wasn't the same little boy I used to know. He responded in a laughing voice, almost like a demonic force, and said,

"No, that's not how you smack him" and proceeded to Smack this kid so hard that he fell asleep before he even hit the ground.

"Oh Shit" ... "Damn…"
"He put that Nigga out" was all the murmurs and whispers I heard from the crowd, but he wasn't done.

Uncle Rome had grown up his entire life with me as a little brother and protecting me. So, to him, it was an insult that the one time he was away from me someone actually tried me, and he made sure to display that. As much as he blamed them, I know he blamed himself because what he did next was just as if not more extreme than the last action. You know how you discipline a child and explain to them while disciplining them why you're disciplining them… Yeah, he did that! He slapped this 6'3 boy until he cried. Keep in mind that my uncle was maybe 5'7, so he literally was jumping each time he slapped him. Imagine taking your open hand and slapping it on a wooden table, that's the sound he made each time he slapped that boy. It had to be a total of 30 times all while explaining to him to never be seen in our area again and telling him to bring both his mother and his father if they had a problem with this. WOW, My Uncle loved me. I knew it before, but I definitely knew it now.

"Let's go home," he said.

I dapped Law before leaving and headed to the house with my uncle.

"You know you're in trouble right" I told him to warn him before he got there.

"I know" he replied but the whole time I was trying to think of a way to get him out of it.

After all, he had just punished these guys for me. His hand was all swollen from slapping the dudes so many times. He really didn't play about me and from that day forward I would never doubt it again. We get to the house and Mima is sitting on the steps outside.

"Where the hell you been?"

I knew she wasn't talking to Uncle Rome, but I immediately answered,

"Some guys just tried to jump me, and Uncle Rome beat them both up."
My Mima was so worried but happy she just hugged us both really tight and said,
"Good."
"Y'all always have to look out for each other," she said.
"Yes ma'am" we replied and headed into the house.
"Y'all hungry?" she asked as we were always hungry.
Again, we replied, "Yes ma'am."
"I'll make y'all some chicken tenders," she said.

Y'all remember the Murray Brand chicken tenders that used to come in the red and black box. Uughhhh, I miss those.

"And put some ice on your hand," she told Uncle Rome.

I knew that his not coming home would get him in trouble but overall, as long as we had one another, that outweighed everything in her eyes. And Uncle Rome was her baby boy, so she was probably looking for a reason not to have to punish him anyway. But this wouldn't be the last of her troubles with my uncle.

Stay tuned!

Red Iversons

I'm a senior y'all!

I'm in the 8th grade. I'm ready to get to high school. My popularity is through the roof, I'm way more confident, and I'm loving every moment of it. A lot of it has to do with joining this step team called Distinguished Gentlemen. Let's back up. All my life I was skinny and when I say skinny, I mean little head, big body, and the wind is blowing me away skinny. I just couldn't gain weight or grow for that matter. I went to visit Mima's family in the South for one summer and now here I am, this fat little husky boy. It was easy to gain weight out there. All they ate was rice, pasta, and cornbread with 4 different kinds of meat for every meal. Sounds crazy I know but it was actually good. I came back a little insecure at first, not knowing how everyone would accept the new me. It was the same as it was last year just with a few extra jokes. Remember when I told y'all I had a love for drums because of my Aunt Elizabeth? Well, last year I met a dude named Francois in a band who convinced me to join a step team. A lot of people confused it with a cheerleading team, we weren't that. We were a step team! Like what fraternities do but way better. I was hesitant but after going to one practice and seeing how the girls flocked to Francois, I knew I had to join. After joining it was just like Francois said but better. I had more girls, I did a lot more traveling, and I was getting the attention I always desired. So, coming back in my 8th grade year a little husky made me nervous but I handled it well if I might say so myself. The Distinguished Gentlemen was a brotherhood. They became a new network of all-aged boys and men to call on in their time of need. At least that's what I thought. The problem with always seeing the good in everyone is that you don't know how to accept that bad when it comes. I traveled the world with this team. Slept on floors with them and protected them in other countries when we were attacked, yes physically, for no reason at all. I say all of that to say this, we were brothers and brothers fight but brothers don't fight to kill. Some of those guys were killers but we're not there yet. So, I'm in 8th grade now. Dating one of the most popular girls in the school. Oh man was she pretty, Light skinned, short so she was my height, and she really liked me. We spent a lot of time together and on the phone. One afternoon she came over and we were chillen. I can still remember it like it was yesterday, I was wearing my red and white Iversons. Don't ask me what else I had on because honestly, it didn't matter, I had on the Iversons. The time came near for her to leave so I walked her to the bus. At the time they were doing construction on the road so the street signs didn't work and the road was horrible. I cross the street from one side of Springfield Boulevard where the park Bello was on to the next with my girl. The bus pulls up, I give my girl a kiss and send her on her way. I'm feeling like the man, my best friend is waiting across the street for me so we can go back to the house and chill. The light turns red, and I proceed to walk and **SMACK!!!** This old bitch hit me with the oldest model Buick I'd ever seen in my life. She hit me so hard I flew in the air like the lady off the intro from the Wayans Brothers show and landed on another car. It sounds bad but the doctor said had it not been for the other car breaking my fall I would've died, when I tell you my shoe was a block away, haha. I'm glad I can laugh about it now. She literally knocked my shoes off my feet. When I came to all I could see was my uncle Rome banging on this old lady's Buick, repeatedly telling her to get the fuck out of the car. He was all wet and had a towel that barely fit wrapped around his waist. I'm glad that the woman didn't get out of the car. My uncle probably would've killed her. Aunt Liz, that's what I started to call my Aunt Elizabeth didn't make it any better when she got there. They wanted all the smoke. But that wasn't the only thing I saw when I came to, Stephon was there. Stephon was my dad. I barely saw my father for a lot of reasons I blamed him for that wasn't solely on him but still. I barely knew this man and he was there. Not days after but minutes after. How? He was there before my mother even knew what happened. Until this day I had only spoken to my dad a total of 7 times and now he was here at a moment when I needed him the most. It was bittersweet but I really wasn't in a place to complain. Hospital, Red Lobster, and then home were the next couple of stops we made. I thought I was good but boy was I wrong. I would only go from the couch to the bed for the next couple of months.

Stay Tuned!

I've Fallen and Can't Get Up

Ouch!!! This Nigga Rome bumped right into my leg. It's been 2 months now that I've been down. I missed my whole summer, but the doctors are feeling really positive about me being up and moving again soon. Just one more MRI and I'm good. I hate those things, but the nurses are really nice to me. I found a solution to the process though... SLEEP. I just go to sleep. So, the day before I stay up as long as I possibly can and then the day of, I knock as soon as I'm in the machine.

"You ready baby" my mother said.

"Yea let's go" I replied.

At one point she was good or at least tried to be. But yeah, off to the doctor we go.

"Randy," one of the nurses said.

They loved me and I liked them. I'm a little horny ass 12yr old who's been cooped up in the house for the entire summer. So, a nice ass in them scrubs is the highlight of my day, week, and month, haha.

"Heeeyyy" I replied.

"You ready for your MRI?" she asked.

"As ready as I can be" I replied.

"Ok Sweetie, Let's go," she said.

I looked at my mother and hopped my ass to the back with that lady to get the MRI over with.

"Randy, we're all done," she said. Damn, how long was I sleep? I know they said I'd be in the machine for 3 hours, but it didn't feel like it.

"Follow me into the room, and the Doctor will be right in," she said.
She took me into a room where my mother was waiting.

"You alright" my mother asked.
"Yea, I'm good" I replied.

Always trying to be strong even when I was scared to death. The last time I was here they told me I'd never walk… run… step again. The fractured hip and how much it had healed was going to take a toll on my life if I didn't get a miracle. In walks the Doctor, this tall man ready to give me good or bad news at any second now.

"How are you feeling?" he asked.

The petty side of me wanted to say how the fuck do you think I'm feeling? I've been in the house for the past 2 months while my friends were enjoying summer. I was on crutches, and I couldn't get comfortable when I slept too afraid to move because of what he diagnosed me with my initial time seeing him, but I just replied.

"I'm good."

"Well, I'm looking at your test, and" he paused.

Nigga if you don't just say it, at this point, I'm nervous but don't play with me either.

"And what" I replied.

"You're all good man," he said.

"We'll just continue to monitor you,

but you can start to walk without the crutches, and we'll get you in some physical therapy and you'll be all set," he said.

I was so overjoyed a tear damn near fell down my face. I was ready to dive back into it.

"So, I can go back to doing everything?" I asked.

"Yes sir, just take it easy. Don't try to do too much" he said.

"Even step?" I replied and that's when he paused.

"Maybe let your body heal 100% before trying to get back into that," he said.

What does that even mean? What's 100%?
Is it when I feel 100%? Is it when you say
I'm 100%? Like what are you talking about?
I just grinned and said,

"OK."

We set up an appointment for the next time I
would see him, and I was out the door. As
soon as we got home, I was outside sitting
on the steps. The minute my friends saw me
they rushed across the street to hear the
news. They were just as excited as I was.
With summer almost over it was about to be
time for high school but now I was meeting
with lawyers. I couldn't even enjoy my last
weeks with my friends.

"We settled on $60,000. That money
will be placed in an account for Randy to
receive when he's 18 years of age but you'll

have access to it in case of Emergency" the lawyer said.

"Ok, Great" Eva replied.

Eva was my mother's name but the series of events that happened after this is when all respect was lost, and she stopped being my mother. I had learned from Uncle Rome that snakes were always in the grass, but I didn't think I'd be the snake's prey at such an early age. I also didn't know that a snake had the capability of eating its young but boy was I about to find out.

Stay Tuned!

The Chicken Wing

Hillcrest mother fucking High School.

I'M… THAT… NIGGA!!

I do what I want when I want, where I want, and how I want. I'm up and out of the house at 7 a.m. waiting for the bus. The Q85 is going to take me to the terminal where I'll go catch the 111 or the 113 to go up the hill if I don't feel like walking. I'm so comfortable at this point, nothing bothers me. By now I've established who I am and I'm not the toughest, but I can definitely hold my own. I've been chillin' with my Uncle Rome and my hot-headed ass cousin Vonte. Vonte was in between the age of Rome and me. He was my Mima's brother's son. Vonte was a mixed black and Chinese breed with long hair. The girls loved him, and he loved himself even more, but he was a fucking psycho. Always ready to shoot or stab someone at the first sight of conflict. I loved him though. He actually was the person who taught me how to rollerblade and play skully. He taught me right there in circle 1 of Rochdale. We had a great bond. So, I'm at school, I walk in, and outside of all the girls there's one face that stands out immediately. Rudy!!! Ight so let's go back real quick, Rudy was a school bully. He bullied me the entire time in elementary school until 4th grade. He had older brothers that were all afraid of my uncle but that didn't stop him from bullying me. Ok, so peep. I'm in 2nd grade in Ms. Frisko's class. It's parent/teacher conference, so my mother decided to go at around 6 right before it ended. She figured the closer we got to the time that it ended, the less people that would be there waiting. We enter the classroom and Ms. Frisko says,

"I'll be right you guys."

"While you wait, show your mom some of your work on the wall" she added.

So, I did as she suggested. When it was our turn to speak to the teacher, she said I didn't need to be there and if I wanted to go to the library I could. So, I wandered off and began heading to the library. After all, if I got lost, I lived directly across the street from the school. While on my way to the library, I see Rudy. Dammit, not Rudy. I hate this guy.

"What you doing?" he said.

"Nothing man. What's up" I replied.

I could already tell he was up to no good. He was in the same class I was in, and his mom was waiting to speak to the teacher which means she wasn't there. She should've had her badass kids with her. This nigga looked and me and didn't say anything else. He just grabbed me and put me in the chicken wing. He swung me from left to right making me look like a fucking puppet. He even started singing and shit.

"Man let me go! I'm not playing Rudy get off me man" I said.

By this time, we were by the stairs the headed towards the library. Do you know

this nigga replied "ok" and flung my ass
down those steps? I felt so helpless and
weak, and I promised myself it would never
happen again. So, you can imagine how
many times I replayed that event happening
in my head. Now I'm standing there, almost
8 years later, and I can remember it like it
was yesterday. I darted straight for this
nigga and grabbed him. Ight so let me
explain. I was little in elementary school,
and I know I said I was established but I had
also grown. I'm about 5'8 now and 170lbs
with a little athletic build and I could fight.
So yeah, it got physical when I saw Rudy. I
expected a fight, some type of tussle or
something. I wanted him to experience this
new and the ass whooping that came along
with it but instead, he just apologized. I just

stood there puzzled. Why was he apologizing? That was weak. I wanted to fight. Instead, he said,

"My bad bro! I was young and dumb. We go back to elementary school." I had lost again. This nigga Rudy took the high road and all I wanted to do was stomp his face in it. I couldn't do anything but walk away and tell him to stay far away from me. I learned a valuable lesson then. I hadn't seen Rudy since elementary school. We went to different Junior high schools. I learned you couldn't hold on to what people used to be because everyone had the ability to change. Whether it be for the best or the worst, the ability is there.

Stay Tuned!

Mr. Funkledick

No one said High School would be this easy. I'm getting to the school at 7:30 a.m. and I'm back at my house by 11 a.m. How Sway? Because I'm leaving after the attendance period. As a matter of fact, I'm leaving as soon as they take attendance. I didn't even wait for the period to end. It started with me just wanting to be home to go to sleep. I was getting up at 5 a.m. to be out of the house by 6 a.m. to make it to school by 7:30 a.m. Keep in mind I wasn't going to sleep every night till about 12 midnight. I'd be tired and falling asleep in class so I figured if I can't be productive here at school, just go home and sleep. Then one day this girl said to me,

"How come I never see you after 4th period?"

I hate that she ever asked me that question because that opened up an entirely new world. First, it started with me just letting her leave with me. Then she asked if one of her homegirls could join and of course, I said "Yes." But then I started realizing I was having these full out, party like, cut sessions. Yooo, I was bugging the fuck out. I was literally getting dressed in the morning just to go to the store to get snacks for the people who would be coming to my house. These people would pay me to come chill with me. A bunch of fucking cool losers or so I thought. See, they were coming when it was convenient for them. Some on Mondays and Thursdays, others on Wednesdays and Fridays but me... I was the host. I was there every day. While they were just slacking on the days, they knew they could slack on, I slacked every day, and then came the phone call. There I am thinking shit is cool. It's Thursday evening and I'm planning the dopest cut party before the weekend starts and in walks my mother.

"Your Vice principal just called and said you've missed damn near the entire school year," she said.

"Nah, he's lying. Couldn't have been me. What days did he say?" I replied. Typical response from a guilty ass kid who's been busted but her reply is what killed me. She said,

"I asked him that and he said it would be easier to tell me what days you were there."

Oh yea, I was fucked. I knew I was in trouble. They were definitely going to flunk my ass. She says,

"I called your father and he'll be attending the meeting with you."

I was so confused. Why would my father be coming to a school meeting with me? I could barely get this nigga in a meeting with me but now he was coming to a meeting at my school. I laughed and replied,

"Oh bet."

See in my mind, he was never going to show up. Plenty of times my dad had made plans with me and not shown up. Ain't no way he was going to find time to meet with my Vice Principal. So, you know what I did right? I kept planning my cut party. I figured if no one showed up then maybe he would think no one cared and that would be the end of it. The next morning comes and I'm up, and I'm ready to party! People already texting and calling me. I even had this lil joint scheduled to come a little earlier so we could smash before the party started. I get up, wash my face, brush my teeth, and then I hear a light knock at the door. I'm hyped now, that got to be my little shawty and I'm about to get some cheeks. I went to the door in some basketball shorts and a tank top on and tried to play it cool. What's up ma?! That's what we used to say back then. But the look she gave me was like she had just saw a ghost and I understood why within the next couple of seconds. My dad had arrived at the same time as the girl. Snuggles was here!

"What's up Dad?" I said

"Nigga don't what's up me?" he replied.

"What are you doing here?" I asked. He gave me the fakest smile looked at the girl and said,

"Sweetheart go home."

"Ran won't be having any company today."

That's when I knew I had fucked up. I didn't know if he was there because he actually cared or because my mother had annoyed him so much that he finally gave in. Either way, I knew it wasn't good because he was there. I get dressed, get in the car and we're off to the school. The entire ride was silent.

He said nothing and neither did I until we pulled up at the school.

"Is there anything I need to know before we go in here?" I contemplated telling him the truth at first, but I didn't know what the outcome would be. See I didn't know him well enough to know how he treated his children. I could've told the truth and got fucked up right in the car and my dad, he wasn't no little guy. So, I just looked at him and said,

"This vice principal stay messing with me. I think he's a racist or something."

Why would my dumbass say that? My dad's eye raised as if he was Huey P. Newton and he had found the Grand Wizard of the Ku

Klux Klan. In a powerful and stern voice, he said,

"Let's go."

Now we're walking up the steps to Hillcrest High and I'm seeing all these people who's supposed to be coming to my party today and they're all trying to speak. One by one I'm signaling for them to shut the fuck up. I couldn't take any chances that the look of anger could go from the Vice Principal to me. We walk through the doors and I'm cracking jokes with Officer Pax. Pax was from the hood, but he worked at the school. He would often be the barrier between me and the teachers whenever we got into it, making sure that no one got disrespected along the way.

"Pax, what's good man" I said.

"Ain't shit man. This ya pops?" He asked.

"Yeah man. We got to meet with Funkledick" I said.

That was a nickname some of the students made up for the Vice Principle.

"Damn man. He looks like he gon' beat yo ass if you in trouble" he said.

"We gon' see" I replied as I walked away to show my dad where the office was.

Now we're waiting. Everyone that passes can see the anger on my dad's face and I can imagine they're thinking that I'm in trouble, but they don't realize this anger is for the racist Grand Master Vice Principle Funkledick. Oh gosh, here he comes.

"Good morning! My name is Mr. Funkleton, and your name is?" He said.

The way my dad replied let me know that I had already won this battle. My dad replied and said,

"Snugs"

That's it! He didn't even give this nigga his real name. He gave him an abbreviation of a nickname. My heart rate had to be above the roof. I couldn't physically show it but in my mind, I was dancing like a fat kid who found a steak in a vegan house. Mr. Funkleton responded with

"Follow me this way into my office".

And my dad replied with

"You're not going to address my son?"

"I'm sorry about that. Good morning Randy." Mr. Funkleton, I replied.

Now we're in the office and the first thing this guy says to my dad is.

"Randy has so much potential. When he does take tests he passes them with flying colors,"

"Ok, then what's the problem?" My dad replied.

"It's his behavior. He can be very disrespectful at times and he's never here" he said.

"How is he never here but he's taking test?" My dad replied.

"He only comes on test days but other than that he's never here" he said.

"That doesn't make any sense. He can't only be here for test days and never here" my dad said.

I was like oh yeah, my dad didn't come to play. I can see my dad was starting to get even more frustrated than he already was, so he changed the subject.

"And what's this about his behavior?" my dad asked.

"He's very disrespectful at times" he said.

My dad looked at me and asked me,

"Is that true?"

Think Randy, Think! I wasn't disrespectful to anyone but him. He had a power trip and the minute you challenged it he went overboard but I knew I was pleasant with everyone else. They always expressed it and I banked on that and won.

"Nah Dad, that's not true at all. You can ask any of the teachers in any of my classes." I said.

"Why is he saying that then" my dad asked.

"Because he gets in our faces and likes to yell and spit on us and act like it's ok. I don't go for it and if you speak out and tell him he shouldn't do that he considers it disrespectful" I said.

"Is that true?" my dad asked Mr. Funkleton.

"Not at all" he replied.

"You can ask anyone, dad. Even some of the teachers have problems with him" I added.

"The bottom line is your son needs to get in line, act like he has some respect, and everything will be fine," he said.

The look my dad gave this man before he verbally assaulted him. Yooo, I had never heard some of these words. My dad started cursing like no one had taught him how to. He was so mad he was stuttering and that's when I knew it was time to go but just like my dad, I had a temper. So here comes Pax to escort my dad out because he knows it's about to get bad and Funkleton says "Get out! You and your badass kid."

While Pax was standing there trying to calm my dad down and explain to him that this vice principal wasn't worth it, there was no one watching me. Before I knew it, I turned around and knocked Funkledick the fuck out. As soon as my fist connected with his face time stopped. Oh shit, what did I do? All I could hear was Pax screaming,

"Get him out of here, go home, and prepare because they're going to call the cops."

I did it this time. Some permanent shit that was going to follow me for the rest of my life. The whole ride home I couldn't think about anything, but I threw my entire life away hitting this principal. Now I'm home just patiently waiting for them to arrive. A day goes by, then the next, then the next, and nothing. Oh, I'm good! And then a letter came in the mail.

Stay Tuned!

G.E.D.

Turns out it wasn't that bad. I didn't get a charge. I was just kicked out of school. Well, actually I was kicked out and banned from attending any District 28 schools which was pretty much all of our high schools. Hillcrest was a good school. I had to be selected to go there. The Blue Ribbon School of Excellence. I used to be proud to say that and somewhere along the line, I didn't even care to say it. Now I was forced with the tasks of finding another school or getting my GED. Well, remember that Distinguished Gentlemen Step team I was a part of the leader had some very good connections and was able to land me a spot in Springfield High School. The same school Uncle Rome went to, but Uncle Rome doesn't attend school anymore. He's straight dealing. All day, every day, to anyone who will buy. The first week in school and everything is going fine. I'm seeing a lot of the people from the neighborhood and it's kind of distracting but I don't care. I'm getting my shit together because I wanna graduate and then it happened. I'm sitting in math class, and I see my uncle Rome knock on the glass. Automatically I think he's there for me, so I walk out of the classroom.

"Oh shit, what's up Nephew," he said. Wait, if he wasn't knocking for me then who? Ain't no got damn way! I see my teacher walk out of the classroom and make an exchange with my uncle.

"Yo, that's my nephew right there," he tells the teacher.

"Make sure he gets a good grade." That's when I knew I would be getting my GED! When Uncle Rome walked out of the school, so did I, and I never looked back. I needed some type of diploma now. I didn't know the first thing about getting my GED. After doing some research I found a school that specialized in helping kids get their GED. Mr. Marvin & Ms. Tracy! They made me feel so at home. I got into this program and it's about 12 of us in the class. It was a small crew which allowed them to help out with us more if we needed it. Everywhere I go I got to start some trouble. There were 2 girls in the class, Ashley & Kate, both baddies. Ashley came from a 2-parent household. She was very classy, and sassy, and wanted to be wined and dined. You can tell she was an only child and was used to being spoiled. She was there because she wanted to be not because she had to be. Kate was the total opposite. Kate was the older sister of 3. Her mother worked as many jobs as possible to make ends meet and Kate handled the kids. She was motherly, and caring, and took time to understand situations. I could relate to Kate, but the chase of Ashley was amusing. Let's just say I made it work. I would date Ashley and then go chill with Kate and the family. It worked for a while until it didn't. Kate needed me more and I understood her lifestyle. I practically raised my brothers and there were times when I wish I had help, but you know. You don't always get what you want. I let Ashley down gently but me and

Kate went on for a while. I helped as much as I could and as much as she would let me. That created an even stronger bond between us but that would be cut short. One evening Kate calls and says we really need to talk. I could sense something was wrong but didn't want to expect anything. She asked if she could come over and because I thought it would just be me and my brothers I said yes. Of course, it ended up being way more people than that due to my mother deciding to come home with friends. Out of all the nights of her coming home and going straight into her room and going to sleep. She decided to want to hang out that night. Kate was here though, and I can tell she really wanted to talk.

"What's up Babe" I said.

"I gotta tell you something," she said.

"You know you can tell me anything." I said.

"My mother's getting married," she said.

I couldn't understand why I would need to know that. Did she need me to attend the wedding with her? That wouldn't be grounds for an emergency though. I was so confused. I just replied,

"Tell her I said congratulations".

"That's not it though," she said.

"Ok, what's up," I said.

"We're moving to Dallas," she said and that's when it made sense. She explained that her mother had found someone who loved her and how much she deserved it. That they were moving to a big house that he owned in Dallas, and it meant a new start. I hated change but I was happy for her. I wasn't even going to try to express having a long distant relationship, so I just told her to be safe and stay in contact. What happened next was imaginable. While all this commotion and laughter was taking place, Kate was saying goodbye to me in the best way. I'm glad none of my mother's friends decided to leave early that night. They would've seen me getting Freaky Freaky! All of that to say when Kate left for Dallas, I left the GED school.

Stay Tuned!

The Bushes

I've lost my girl, and I still don't have a diploma. Uncle Rome is locked up and I'm all in these streets alone. He left me a little bit of protection though. It was shiny, short, and held 6 rounds. Man, I took that .22 caliber with me everywhere I went. Kept that little thing right in my pocket. One day I go to the store to get a sandwich and on my way back I get pressed by some young niggas.

"Run your pockets nigga" one of them said.

He can't be talking to me. They're literally about to try to jump me and I'm going to lay all three of them down. No gun, no knife. They were really old school in a new school era. I just laughed and told them to keep it pushing. Turns out we had some new gang rivals in the area, and they hated me. They heard all about my uncle and me and wanted whatever static I was ready to provide.

"Run that shit nigga" another one said. I take a deep breath, hand already in my pocket to pull out my .22, and right before I do I hear,

"Nah, he's good."
Immediately these little dudes stepped off.

"You good ?" he asked.

"I'm straight" I replied before walking off.

As I continued to walk back to the house, I noticed that he was following me. Now I'm taking precautions. I'm crossing the street but still going in the same direction. I wanna go home but I don't know what the dude's intentions were. He could've called off the small dogs just to finish the job himself and the last thing I wanted this dude to know was where I lived. As I approached my block, he gave me the peace sign and headed towards my house. I lived in a 2-family home. My door on the right leads to an upstairs 3-bedroom, 2-bathroom apartment. The door on the left was the same but just on the main floor.

"Yooo where you going?" I asked.

"Home" he replied.

Just as he said that I saw the big U-Haul truck in front of my house. Did this nigga bring gang members with him to the neighborhood he moved to? Ain't no way he had clout like that. Turns out he was always from the neighborhood. He was just low-key and wasn't in my age group, so I didn't know him like that.

"I guess we're neighbors" I said.

"I guess so." He replied.

"Randy," I said.

"Heavy" he replied.

Little did I know that the stranger who stopped the altercation earlier would become my neighbor, friend, and ultimately my brother. We built a bond so tight that at 1 point it was impossible to see one without the other. 2 brothers of the opposite gang always together confused a lot of people. I know they had a lot to say but didn't dare but the ones that did were met with mayhem. We weren't the guys you wanted to fuck with. So, one night we're at a lounge and Heavy and another one of our partners Eric decide that they don't like the party, so they leave. I stayed because the person throwing the party was a good friend of mine and I wanted to show support. While we're at this party we get into it with this dude. He doesn't realize that almost the entire party knows each other. We schemed and plotted on this dude to fuck him up when he came outside but we were so drunk that we allowed him to hear the plan. He really helped us plan it. Once he realized it was about him, he walked away and went straight to his car. He was gone. Boy did we feel dumb but when Heavy and Eric got word, they came up there to see what was going on. By this time the party was over, but we weren't done.

"Let's go back to the other spot," Heavy said.

So, we got in the car and headed over there. When we arrived all the lights were on and everyone in the club was fighting. I just stood there in amazement at first watching people get knocked out left and right. Until I noticed that one of the guys fighting was someone, I knew from that Distinguished Gentlemen team I had been a part of years ago. As soon as I went to engage in the physical activities Heavy grabbed me.

"This ain't our fight bro," he said. I just stood there upset. Most of the time I listened to Heavy because he had my best interest at heart at all times. But then I noticed someone from the hood getting jumped and I guess that's when Heavy felt it was ok to help out. Imagine getting involved in a club fight and saying hey I don't wanna fight, I'm just trying to get my homeboy off the floor. Haha. It was a joke, at least that's what they took it as when Heavy tried to do it. Heavy started flinging guys one by one off this dude from our hood and then it happened. SMACK! Someone hit Heavy. He looked at Eric and me and said,

"Let's fuck them up."

and we did just that. Heavy started knocking niggas out left and right. I planted myself on the stage and proceeded to field goal kick every person that Heavy didn't knock out. Eric was smacking niggas with chairs. It was Epic. We were fucking the entire club up and then it hit us. Oh, Shit, we're fighting the entire club. It's only 3 of us. Even the dudes that we were in this fight for left us. 50 dudes in the club from the same hood against 3 of us. The hood still talks about that fight. We held our own. All Heavy kept saying was don't hit the ground. We were getting busy until we weren't. Things started to shift. It's like they called more people to come and join in the fight. Next thing I know I had a nigga playing peek-a-boo with a bottle upside my head. Heavy was cut across his face and had a black eye and Eric was still chasing Niggas with this chair he found. But I knew I had my .22 in the car. So, I fought all the way out of the club and to the car. I thought if I could just get my hands on it, they're going to be sorry. Now I'm tired and they're fucking me up but I'm at the car. Y'all are going to be sorry now! I go to open the trunk it's locked, and I don't have the key. Damn back to square one… Keep fighting. What I'm about to tell you is funny as hell, but it wasn't funny then. These niggas grabbed me. Some by my hands and the others by my feet and they threw my ass in a thorn bush. The only thing that saved me was they heard the sirens and took off. I managed to grab my phone and call my sister Dusse. When she arrived, I was fucked up. Let me paint the picture for you. I walked in this party wearing red and white uptowns with blue and red Evisu jeans. I had on a white T-shirt and a red leather jacket. When I left, I was wearing all red. Every item of clothing I had on that was white was now red from the blood that was gushing out of my head. I was really fucked up. I was out of it, but I remember seeing Eric come out in handcuffs. Heavy on the other hand came out cuffed to a stretcher. What the fuck happened from the time I went to get the gun? I was pissed.

"Let's go, Let's go," my sister Dusse said to our homeboy Tory as he cried in the car. He even asked me to put on a hat because the car was a rental. This Nigga! 21 stitches I had to get and a cast for my broken finger. All I could think about was when Heavy and Eric were getting released and getting revenge. Revenge on the niggas that ran and left us and the niggas that did this to us. I didn't have to though. Karma always comes back full circle. I was watching the news and saw the same dude that was hitting us with the bottles. Turns out he was stabbed to death by his baby's mother the very next morning after the fight. The night he was fighting us, she thought he was with another girl. Won't GOD do it.

Stay Tuned!

Where's my Money?

It's my mother fucking birthday. Today I turn 18! I was out drinking all night last night with the homies. They really showed out for your boy. Shot after shot, bottle after bottle. They made sure I was super drunk, but I was safe. The entire block came out and we just blasted music and chilled among friends. Now I have a headache and I'm hungry. Heavy and I came and went in each other's house as if it were our own. I trusted him more than I had trusted anyone else around me at the time.

"Yooo Heavy!" I screamed. Hoping he was upstairs and not downstairs at his crib.

"Yooo" he answered.

"I'm hungry bro," I said.

"Shit, me too" he replied.

I just laughed. Heavy wasn't the brother to handle everything, he was just always there.

"What we gon eat nigga" I said before getting up and walking into the kitchen. My eyes had to be playing tricks on me. There were niggas all over my house. I know my mother saw all of them before leaving the house.

"Heavy what the fuck! Why are all these people in my house?" I asked.

"You should see my crib" he responded.

I had seen enough.

"Wake up!! Wake the fuck up! Y'all gotta go!" I screamed.

Everyone complained and got grumpy except this one girl. She just got up, grabbed

98

her things, and dipped. I had seen her around but didn't know her name.

"Yooo where you going," I asked.

"You just said everyone needed to go" she just snapped back at me.
Now I'm trying to think of a way to keep her here.

"You weren't going to offer to help clean" I asked.

"I got you bro," Heavy said.
I just looked at him.

"I'm not talking to you Heavy" I replied. Then everyone else decided to be helpful.

"We got you, bro."

"We'll clean before we head out"
I started hearing all these helpful cock blocking niggas who wasn't getting the hint

to get the fuck out of my house. After seeing
the frustration on my face, she said

"If you wanted me to stay, that's all
you had to say."
Oh Shit, I really liked her personality.

"I want you to stay" I said.

"Ok cool. Where's your room?" she
said.
I pointed her in the direction of my room
and watched her walk in there and close the
door. Who the fuck was this girl and why
she's so confident?

"Heavy, who's that?" I said.

"That's Shawna, she lives right by the
Pathmark" he responded.
That's all I needed to know. I didn't care if
she had a man because if it was important,
he would've told me. After everyone

cleaned up and left, I was still hungry and had this girl in my room doing only GOD knows what. She could've been stealing all my stuff. I get to the door and knock.

"Can I come in?" I asked.

I heard nothing. So, I knocked again but harder.

"Yooo, you good?" I asked.

Still nothing. I wasn't in the mood for any surprises. I tried to be a gentleman, but I was aggravated at this point. I just opened the door, and she was lying in my bed, under the covers playing on her phone.

"You didn't hear me knocking on the door?" I asked.

"Yea I heard you, but I figured whoever was knocking didn't belong in here. Who knocks to come in their own room?" She said.

"I was trying to be respectful," I said.

"By not coming in your room?" She asked.

Oh my God! She was such a smart ass, and this would be the first of many conversations that we would have like this. So, as we bickered back and forth, me still standing and her in my bed she asked

"Why are you still standing up?"

"I don't know" I responded.

"Are you nervous? Do I scare you?" she asked.

Imagine that! I just nodded yes sarcastically before sitting down on the bed.

"Yooo I'm hungry," I said.

"What do you want to eat" she asked with the weirdest little grin on her face.
I was down to fuck, but I definitely wasn't eating the box. I didn't know shawty. I just looked at her and said,

"What you cooking". And little to my surprise she answered and said.

"Whatever you want."
She was serious. She was about to cook for your boy but what was in my fridge? My mother was never home and even when she was, we always ordered takeout. I had money but I was tired of takeout. I looked at her and shrugged my shoulders saying,

"I don't know what's in the fridge".

"Let's go to my house and then we can go to Pathmark and get something," she said.

That worked for me, so we got up, got dressed, and headed to her house. When we arrived, there was no one there. I expected to see a parent or something but no one. She told me to get comfortable and make a list of what I wanted to eat. Why would I be making a list if we were going to the store together? Because we weren't. She showed me to her room and had me get in the bed and handed me a remote.

"I'll be right back."

 I know damn well this girl didn't just leave me in her house. She must live alone I thought. Ain't no way you just going to leave someone in your house knowing that someone could potentially walk in and see me here. I didn't know and honestly, I didn't care at the moment. I was 18 years old

today. Today was the day I cashed in.
$60,000 from that car accident lawsuit. I
pick up the phone and call my mother.

"Happy Birthday Baby," she said.

"Thanx Ma," I said.

"What you doing" she asked.

"At some girl house," I replied.
I didn't lie to my mother. I didn't feel the
need to at this point in my life. I was
unapologetically me.

"Ugh, Ran what girl? Do you even
know her name?" she asked.

"That doesn't matter right now Ma. I
need to know the information to get my
money" I said.

"What money?" she asked.

"My money from my settlement" I
responded.

My mother got quiet. I knew something was up, but I didn't know what to expect. I thought maybe she had spent some of it. I didn't know for sure though.

"Ma you there?" I asked.

"I'm here" she replied.

She told me the name of the bank and I remembered it from the documents, but she said she had to check and make sure everything was open for me to get it. It didn't sound right. She started dancing with her words and stuttering. I was getting a very bad feeling. So, I told her we'd figure it out later when we were together but, in my head, I already knew I had some digging to do. As soon as I got off the phone, I called a family friend whose mother was the manager at the bank, who then connected me with her. What she told me would change my life forever. I had no money. Not one dime. My money had been gone a year after that account was opened. My mother and I had plenty of conversations about that money and she'd known for years that it was gone. What did you spend $60,000 on? I was so lost. I wasn't mad that she spent it, I was more upset that she lied all these years to me. Damn, I needed to be alone. I got up and grabbed my jacket and headed out the door. When I opened the door, I was met by this elderly woman who was about to enter.

"Who are you" she asked.

"Hey. I'm Shawna's friend" I replied. She was trying to carry all these bags, so I jumped in and assisted. I told y'all I was raised by my grandparents, and I had manners.

"Oh, thank you," she said.

"No problem at all" I replied.

"Can you tell Shawna I had to leave please?" I asked.

"Yea, I will. Where is she" she asked.

"She went to the store real quick" I responded.

"It was a pleasure meeting you." I added before walking off and that's when she stopped me.

"Come here," she said.

I was so lost.

"Ma'am" I replied.

"Come here," she said.

So, I entered and closed the door. She just stared at me for 2 mins and said, "what's wrong?" I was stuck.

I didn't know what to say to this lady. I just wanted to leave. I wanted to get back to my house and wait for my mother to arrive so I could curse her out. I damn sure wasn't about to tell this lady that I didn't know what was going on.

"Sit down," she said.

"I really need to go" I responded.

"No, you don't," she said.

She told me that she could see I was about to go do something that I was going to regret later. She was probably right but I needed to get that anger out of me.

"You're not like the rest. You're a good one" she said.

I didn't know what she meant then, but I would learn exactly what it meant. Just as she's about to say something else Shawna enters in.

"When did you get home" she asked.

"Maybe about 10mins ago" the lady replied.

"Hey, I'm going to head out. I have some business to handle" I said.
 Shawna gave me the same look the lady did.

"Ma can you give us a minute" she said to the lady.

"Oh, that's your mom? She was really nice." I said.
Shawna just continued to stare at me. I didn't know what to do so I let her stare for a couple of more minutes before saying.

"Ight, I'm going to head out"

When I went to get up, she pushed me back down. Ain't no way this girl was about to try to fight me because I wanted to leave.

"Something's wrong and I'm not letting you leave until I can see you're good," she said.

"I'm good," I said.

"Nah, it's your birthday and I can see it all over you that you're not good," she said.

Then she proceeded to pull me into her room, climbed on top of me, and just laid on top of me. What the hell was going on? I had people calling and texting me to do shit for my birthday and I couldn't leave. Let me be honest, I didn't want to leave. I knew she was right. I was upset, hurt, confused, angry, and sad on the one day I should've been the happiest. So, I stayed because she made me feel like the only person that mattered in the world. For the next 2 weeks or so I was there. I bought some basketball shorts and some underclothes and just stayed there. She fed me, fucked me, washed my clothes, and made sure I needed for nothing. She had no job but had all this money. I didn't know where she was getting it from, and I didn't care. Her mother would pop in occasionally and just make sure we were good but most of the time it was like she wasn't even there. Maybe she wasn't. Finally, the time came, and I was ready to leave. I told her I'd be back, and she expressed that whenever I was ready the door would be open. We didn't put a title or anything on what we had, it just worked.

I'm home now in what appears to be a ghost town. It was as if no one had been there since I left until I went into my room and noticed a handwritten letter from my mother. The letter stated how sorry she was for spending all of my money. She said she didn't mean to hurt me, and that she would begin trying to pay all of it back. She explained what she purchased with some of the money, and this made me even more angry. Furniture for your sister and laptops for friends. You splurged my money on your people. $60,000 of my money was spent on your sister and your friends. I told myself I would wait. I needed more… I need answers. This wasn't enough. I needed her to come home so we could have this talk face to face but the more I looked at this letter, the angrier I got. Then it happened. I fucked the house up. I looked at the TV and thought did she purchase this with my money and boom… TV broke. Then the dressers, then the walls in the apartment, and so on. I broke and trashed everything in the house until the hurt in my heart fell from my eyes in tears. After it was all done, I knew it was time for me to go. My mother or Eva as I would call her from here on out had changed me. I would trust no one ever again. The biggest snake in my life had become the one who birthed me. And this was far from being the last time she would do it.

Stay Tuned!

Monopoly

18 and out of control. I've reached the point where any and everything is acceptable. I've even started chilling with some new people. Well not really new. I went to elementary school with this kid, and we talked here and there but he wasn't someone I really considered a friend. We lived in the same hood and see each other from time to time but we weren't close like that until one day as adults we decided to chill. And low behold, we were more alike than we thought. He became friends almost immediately and would hangout regularly. His name was Christopher, but we called him Ears as a nickname because his ears were large. Most of the time it was the first thing you noticed about him. Ears and I bonded over women. We would bag girls

who had a crew and run through them. That was our thing. One night while chilling we got a call from one of the girls who said they're crew wanted to chill. Cool, let's set it up. We cleaned the basement, headed to the liquor store, and waited for the girls to arrive. When they arrived, we got right to it. Let's play a drinking game. In this game we would ask questions to see who wanted who and how the night was going to go. After all, they weren't there to just chill. A few rounds of Bacardi 151 later and we are ready to go. We all went to our locations and started to do what horny teenagers did. Something didn't seem right though. I could tell we were being plotted on. Eyes of the girls wandered across the room as they just watched what the other couple was doing. I could tell they were up to something but didn't know what. My thoughts were, they were going to rob us but that never happened. When we were done, they laughed and joked for a while and then headed out. Another win for Ears and me. We didn't have to take them out to dinner or have random ass conversations. All it took was a game, a bottle of 151, and the fact that they already knew what they wanted. What more could a man ask for? We always had a rule anyway. The minute any female would act as if they didn't know if they wanted to, the night was over. We never wanted anyone to feel forced into anything. We were gentlemen. A few nights passed and on this particular night Ears and I weren't together. I was at a birthday gathering for some other associates of mine. I was drunk! And not just regular drunk, I mean stumbling to the door, coaching myself home, & laying on the steps drunk. I finally make it in the house and my phone rings. I'm thinking it's the people I just left checking in to make sure I made it home. It definitely wasn't them.

"Hey," the caller said.

"Who's this" I replied.

"It's Felicia," she said. Even if I knew who she was I probably wouldn't have known this night.

"Who" I replied.

"The girls from the other night," she said.

119

That didn't help me at all. We went through plenty of women all the time, but I was drunk, so I just said.

"Oh, OK"

Although I was drunk, I wasn't dumb enough to not realize that it was 1 or 2 a.m. She barely knew me so the only reason she would be calling was to fuck.

"What you doing" she asked.

"Literally just got home" I replied.

"You sound smacked," she said.

"I'm ight" I said.

After she made that comment I could hear someone in the background saying

"Tell him, tell him."

"Tell me what?" I asked.

"Oh, you can hear her?" She said before laughing.

120

"Yea I can," I said.

We wanted to know if you wanted to come over and play Monopoly" she said. Now any other day I'm down. Monopoly was and still is one of my favorite games but today I was too drunk. There was no way I was going to be able to focus let alone keep my eyes open.

"Nah, I'm too drunk to play monopoly," I said.

"I thought you said you wasn't drunk," she said.

"I never said that."

"Just come over. I'll call you a cab" she said.

She didn't even know my address, but I must have given it to her somewhere in that conversation because 10 minutes later I was in a car on my way to wherever she was. Upon arrival, I was greeted at the door and helped up the stairs. I knew I heard 2 females. One was light skin and tall and the other brown and short. I asked myself in my head over and over again what I was doing there but it was too late at this point. I was here and whatever was going to happen was going to happen. I just hoped that I'd live to tell this story that I'm telling right now. After we got up the stairs, they took me in a room. No way were these girls about to rape me. As soon as the door opened, I saw the monopoly board set up and money was already distributed. They really wanted to play Monopoly at 2 am. This was too weird but fuck it, I'll try. We're 10 minutes into the game and I'm starting to sober up. I told y'all I loved this game but right as I'm sobering up here comes the shots.

"Nah I'm good," I said.

"You gotta take some shots with us," Felicia said.

"Don't be no punk" the light skin one added

Damn! I couldn't be no punk, so I started taking shots. I rolled an 8… Yes! I got Boardwalk. Just as I said that Felicia flipped the board. I thought she was mad because I got it first but that's when it happened. She took my hat off my head and put it on hers and they both begin to undress me. Oh Shit, I'm about to have a Monopoly 3 some. They took turns having their way with me and I didn't complain. Well, I did once but that's because I sat on one of those little green houses and it stuck me in my ass. I woke up the next morning and didn't remember anything. I could hear laughter as they watched what appeared to be a video of me. They thanked me for coming and got me out of there quickly. That was when I realized females were worse than niggas. I had a new appreciation for women and monopoly for that matter. I never got that hat back and if I ever see that video I'm suing.

Stay tuned!

Long Island

The Ears and I era was crazy. We did it all. The girls were just a portion of our story. Ears was always into some shit. One night we're traveling to go see these girls in Long Island. This was a 45-minute to an hour trip by car, but we hoped it would be worth it. Ears was a part of this car gang called the Civic Boyz. Back then this was a thing, your crew only drove this particular brand of vehicles and they would often race other crews, such as the Toyota Boyz, and whatever else brand name crew was out there. Lame, yeah, I know. That was his thing though, so he was always speeding. I didn't mind most time times though because an hour trip would turn into 30 minutes. I would always tell him just get me there safe. This particular night he decided to do the speed limit to get the girls. We would talk details on how we met the girls, their names, and some of the conversations. We did this just to make sure that we didn't mix them up with any of the other girls in our lives. Haha! We've arrived to get the girls with the intention that we would be hanging out there. We were wrong! They came out with their jackets on and their purses in their hands. Ears and I both looked at each other and then at them confused.

"What's the plans, ladies?" I asked.

"What you mean" one of them replied.

"I thought we were hanging out here." Ears said to them.

"Change of plans," the other girl said.

"My mom is having company," she said.

Ears looked frustrated. There was no way he had driven out here just to turn around and drive back to Queens. Then he would have to turn around and bring them back that same night. With a frustrated look on his face, he said

"Maybe we should reschedule because I'm not driving to Queens and bring y'all back tonight".
They just looked at each other and smiled.

"Who said anything about coming back tonight?" one of them replied.
They were down for the cause. They probably were more prepared than we were. After looking more closely, I noticed that one of them had her toothbrush sticking out of her bag. She had done this before. Ears

realizing what type of night it was going to be smiled and said,

"We out!" before pulling off aggressively.

Now he's in a good mood and in a rush to get back to the house. So, guess what he's doing? 120 mph! Like I said earlier I didn't care as long as he got us to our destination safely. And that's when it happened. I saw the blue lights. We were being pulled over by the police. You know that rumbling feeling you get in your stomach when something bad is about to happen? Almost like you have to take a shit... Yup, I had that feeling. I know I definitely farted. I knew my gun was somewhere in this car. We were about to go to jail and to make matters worse I wouldn't get to smash the new girl.

Before I could scream it, I heard Ears blurt out "Fuck!" Aww Shit, that wasn't good. That means he also had some illegal shit in the car as well. With a defeated look on my face, I asked.

"What's in the car?"

"I just picked up that package and meant to take it home before picking up the girls, but we didn't have time." He answered.

Now we were looking at a gun charge and a possession charge. Rikers here we come. I had always heard stories about it but had never been. In the streets, you always had to put on a face like you weren't worried about shit like that but in all honesty, I knew myself and everyone else around me was afraid of going there. We knew niggas who went there and didn't come home or came back with permanent face scars. I considered myself to be a handsome young man. I didn't want any extra scars that I wasn't born with. Here comes this officer with his hand already on his gun. This wasn't going to be good. I could already see it because Ear's tents were so dark, we already had the windows down.

"License and Registration," the officer asked.

Ears handed him everything.

"Do you know why I'm pulling you over?" the officer asked.

Ears being a smart ass responded.

"Because you wanted my autograph?" with this silly ass smirk on his face. I wanted to smack the entire front row of teeth out of his mouth, but I held my composure.

"Funny Guy. I'll be right back" he said.

When he walked away, I damn near killed Ears with the look I gave him.

"Yooo Chill," I said.

"What I do" he replied.

I clenched my teeth and repeated.

"Chill!"

You know the way parents used to talk to their child when they couldn't beat them right there because there were too many people around. It's safe to say he got the point because when the office came back his entire demeanor changed. I could tell he was just as nervous as I was, but I wouldn't show mine. I had a reputation, but I had more to lose. He would've had a little possession charge but me, I was going down for this firearm. The officer returned to the car and said,

"Everyone out of the vehicle"
That's when I noticed that he had a partner. Aww damn, it was about to happen. Once I saw that second cop car appear I knew we were going down. You know what they say, two cop cars and someone's definitely going to jail. Here we are in the middle of January with no jackets on and there's snow on the ground. They had us standing outside while they trashed the car. I saw shorts and sneakers on the wet ground. They tossed out our bottle of 151 we had just purchased from the liquor store. They were even throwing out the change that was in the cup holder.

You could see the steam coming from the car. I couldn't tell if it was from the cold air or how mad they were from not being able to find anything. Finally, they said.

"You can go" before handing Ears a ticket.

I just looked at Ears surprised and told the girls get in the car. I started to pick up the shorts and the sneakers to put them in the trunk before Ears said.

"Fuck that shit. We out"

Say less!

I was ready to go but apparently, he was more ready than I was. The ride back to the house was quiet. We both were trying to figure out how we got out of this. We didn't want to talk about it on the way home and jinx ourselves, so we just thought about it.

When we pulled in the driveway Ears and I both smiled. We couldn't hold in our excitement anymore.

"Bro" I yelled.

Before I could say anything else he put a code in the radio and that shit opened up. This nigga had a safe-like radio. This BMF ass, secret compartment having genius. We laughed so hard we damn near cried. Then I started looking for my gun but I couldn't find it. Where the hell was my gun? No way I lost it. Maybe the cops had thrown it out when they were searching the car so hard. I couldn't even be mad. I wasn't in jail, and we were safely back at the house with these girls who wanted to celebrate this win with us. Good thing we always had a backup bottle of 151 at the house because the liquor store was closed at this point. A week later I'm chilling with my sister. She looks at me and says,

"Are you missing something?"
I thought about it, but I couldn't remember so I just responded.

"Nah, I don't think so. Why what's up?"
She reached into the back seat and handed me my brown Sean Jean jacket. The jacket seemed heavier than usual. Oh, Shit, she found my gun.

"Where you find it at?" I asked.
Then she began to tell me how I left her car one warm day. She told me our little brother noticed it and asked.

"Is that Randy's jacket?" with a confused look.

When she responded

    "Yea"

he just looked at her and said.

    "Put that shit in the trunk."

    "Why" she asked.

    "Randy always got something on him," he said.

And as sure as the sun rises, he was right. My sister had it the whole time. I looked at her, smiled, and hugged her. She didn't understand why I was hugging her. I'm pretty sure she thought it was because she had my gun, but it was way more. The more she explained why my jacket was left in the car, the more I understood. We were drinking and I was hot because she was blasting the heat. It was wintertime but she always did everything to an extreme. When it was hot, she blasted the AC. When it was cold, she blasted the heat. When she drank, she got drunk. My sister and her extremities saved my life. At least it did this time. We didn't go back to Long Island for a while after that. If those girls wanted to see us, they found their way to us.

Stay tuned!

Dusse

My father had a lot of kids. Some I knew and some I didn't. Between both parents, I had more brothers than I could count and 6 sisters. I only acknowledged one sister though… Dusse. My one and only sister if you let me tell it. I see the other ones in passing and even on social media but she's the only one that matters to me. You could tell me that one of my sisters was on fire and I'd respond as long as it ain't Dusse. We nicknamed Dusse after her love for the drink. I would say her real name but she's way too popular for that and she would beat me up. Dusse is aggressive, overprotective about what and who she loves, and very outgoing. She's the life of the party. She's a friend to many and has very few enemies. She's the give you the shirt off of her back but don't piss her off person. She's like the female version of the Incredible Hulk… Dr. Jekyll and Ms. Hyde. Shawty will flip on you! Dusse and I have been schooling together from Day 1. After all, she's only older than me by 2 months. We played basketball as kids growing up. Dusse was as dope in ball then as she is now. It's like she knew she was supposed to be a basketball player. One day in 2nd grade we were playing basketball outside during recess, we were playing 3 on 3 on concrete. The people who picked the teams always picked me last because I was small. I always got picked though because I could shoot. Dusse on the other hand was a power forward. She'd drive to the hole knocking down any and everyone who got in her way. Remember I told y'all she was aggressive right? I had this big head nigga on my team named Ron. He wasn't really that good, but he could handle the ball. This one day he was scoring and all. He was really getting the best of the other team. Dusse didn't like that. She started to foul him and push him into the gate. She turned into a real bully.

"Stop fouling him," I said.

"Stop crying," she told me. She knew she was wrong but wasn't about to let me tell her what to do. The next couple of plays were even worse but she would foul him to get a rise out of me.

"Stop fucking fouling him before I foul you," I said.

"Do it" she replied.

"Let's go, Time to go inside" the teacher begins yelling to us. I was saved by the bell. I was little as fuck in elementary school. I probably weighed no more than 40lbs. I knew Dusse would've beat my ass. We're in class now and I left it all on the basketball court. I turn around to say something to Dusse and she's staring at me like she wants to kill me. Dammit! She was still mad. The teacher called out for art time, and it was time to go color. I walked over to my sister to smooth things out and asked.

"What you coloring?"

She looked at me and said.

"I'm going to fuck you up."

I know what you're thinking. They were cursing at an early age. Hell, yeah we were but only to each other. You know how little

143

kids were about things they weren't supposed to do. We loved doing it outside of the presence of adults of course. After Dusse said that to me I responded with

"I'll hit you in the head with a lock." I didn't even have a lock, but I thought if I threatened her she'd chill. Why do I do that? She pushed out from her desk, jumped down and proceeded to grab me. I put my little feet to work that day. Throwing kids in front of me and all that to get away from her. There was this big girl in our class named Theresa. I used to call Theresa all types of names as a child. Theresa was at least 6'1 and 200 lbs as a 2nd grader. We had a weird relationship though. I would call her names and she pick me up by my pants and shake me. I would come to find out later on in life she was our sister as well. One of our father's kids. As I was running to get away from one sister, I bumped into the next.

"Move your big cholesterol eating ass Theresa," I said.
And as usual, she grabbed my little ass, picked me up and started shaking me.

"Put me down Big Debra," I said. Making reference that she had eaten too many little Debbie snacked that she turned into Big Debra. That was a clever joke for a 2nd grader. As she shook me Dusse caught up to me. Damn, they were about to jump me or so I thought.

"Put my brother down now," Dusse said.
No one played with Dusse. Her aggression and delivery made a statement that told you

145

that she'd beat your ass. No matter how big or strong, if you fucked with Dusse you were going to have a problem. Theresa immediately put me down and walked away. She didn't want no problems. Being the little jerk that I was I began to taunt her.

"Yea... You don't want no problems with my sister. Walk away Giant" I said. Before I could turn around and say thank you or sorry Dusse had me in the headlock. It took 2 teachers to get her off me. She didn't get in any trouble for it either. The teachers heard me talking shit to Theresa and thought Dusse was defending her. She actually got an extra snack that day, My snack. They went over the no tolerance for bullying procedures and informed my Mima that if it happened again, I would be suspended. That day I got a wedgie from Theresa, choked out my Dusse, and my Mima was waiting at the door for when I got home with one of my grandfather's real leather belts. I learned a valuable lesson that day. Don't get caught! I would continue to talk shit for the rest of my life, but I strived on the ability to do it without being caught. It may not have been the right lesson to learn but it was the lesson I learned.

Stay tuned.

BBQ on Edgewood

Summertime was epic in our neighborhood. That's when we would all rally up and throw the most extravagant BBQs on Edgewood. Edgewood was the block I spent most of my older teen years and twenties on. The place where I felt the most safest. One Saturday morning, after having a long liquored Friday night, we decided that the party needed to continue. Yup, it was time for a BBQ. We started calling up all the key people to get it done. Our key people were our friends and family that did the behind the scenes shit. They did the cooking, cleaning, put up money for the food, and so on and so on. And then you had people who just got invited. Some were also family and friends, but they weren't doing shit. They were lazy and unreliable. You couldn't count on these niggas to bring a soda. Anyway, after everything was set into motion and everyone was informed, it was time to have a drink. That's mostly what the summer consisted of, fun and drinks. Dusse always had some type of concoction that she was brewing up in her room. This time it was a mixture of Corn Liquors, but we'll get back to that. Everyone has arrived and we're having a good time. There was even ppl here that we didn't invite but it's whatever. We have enough food and drinks and that's all that matters. While we're chilling outside, we see our long-time childhood friend Bobby that we haven't seen in a long time. We met Bobby in elementary school. He became a friend, and we kept the relationship ever since. When Bobby turned 18, he started getting

crazy in them streets. He started building a
reputation that even we couldn't understand
but Bobby was doing all of this secretly.
Bobby came from a 2 parent household and
his father wasn't having it. He made Bobby
enlist in the army as soon as he got word of
what he was doing. And just like that Bobby
was gone and heading in the right direction.
That meant we didn't see much of Bobby
but when we did, we made sure to enjoy our
time together. We had so many questions,
curious and wanting to know how our friend
was doing but our evening would be
interrupted by unfamiliar assholes. We
always had a rule on the block that random
couldn't just invite people. Most of the time
we turned people away but because we were
so excited about Bobby, we just let it slide.

It would come back to haunt us. While we were in deep conversation, we noticed a dude sitting on Bobby's car.

"Yooo, my man can you not sit on the car," Bobby said.

"Oh, my bad" he replied. Ok cool, he got the memo. Don't sit on Bobby's car. Why would you be sitting on anyone else's property anyway? People had no respect, but we let it rock because we noticed he was one of Short Sleeve's friends. Short Sleeve was this girl who was always around. She also went to school with us but to this day I still couldn't understand why she was always around. She had no real ties to anyone on the block. This evening she decided to invite some friends. Sketchy, weird, and disrespectful people. 10 minutes into our conversation, Bobby notices the dude sitting on his car again.

"Yooo, please get off my car man," he said.

"Oh Damn, my bad," the dude said. And that's when it happened, all I heard was.

"He's going mad hard, It's not that serious."
That's when Dusse and I decided to chime in. Bobby was our guest and he asked politely twice for you to get off his property, which to us was way too many times. By not respecting his wishes meant that you were disrespecting us. Before I could say anything Dusse started flipping.

"Stay the fuck off his car! It is that serious Nigga" she said.

Short Sleeve looked at Dusse and said.

"It's not that serious."

and that's when Dusse instructed her to leave or both her and her company would get fucked up. See we were really friendly people until you pushed us too far. We'd party with you all day but don't disrespect or cross us. After all the commotion we decided to have some drinks and start some shit talking.

"I can out drink anyone here," I said. I haven't mentioned my little brother OG yet. He's the anything you can do, I can do better little brother. We were always in completion but in a good, friendly, brotherly way. OG walked over and screamed.

"Bullshit"

and that's when it started. We started going shot for shot. We went through the Patron bottle first and then made our way to the Henny. Before we knew it, we had drunk everything. There was no more liquor to prove our point. Oh, but there was.

"Dusse go get the corn liquor," OG said.

Dusse curious to see how drunk her concoction would get hurried to get the mixture and gave me a shot. OG tapped out but my dumbass…. I'm taking this shot. While all this is going on my little cousin comes and tells me that some dude at our BBQ is being wild disrespectful and trying to talk to his girl. He couldn't remember exactly what the dude looked like but what he did remember was a "red hat" the guy was wearing. No team, No logo… just a "Red Hat". The entire party stopped, and we began looking for the guy in the red hat. I sent guys up the block, we searched the backyard, and even called around looking for the guy in the "Red Hat". It was about to go down. No one was going to disrespect my family at one of our BBQs.

"Find this nigga" I yelled out. Ears is next to me making sure I'm good because I had just taken that damn Corn Liquor. After about 30 minutes of looking for this dude and not finding him, we concluded that maybe the dude had just taken off. I'd find out who he was another time, and we'd take care of him but right now I needed to lay down. I didn't know every liquor mixed in Dusse's concoction but what I did know was the room was spinning and it wouldn't stop even with my eyes closed. I never drank anything from Dusse again unless I saw her open the bottle fresh. The next morning, I felt horrible. This hangover was real, and we still had to go outside and clean up from last night's festivities. But not before Dusse and OG entered the room with some information.

"Bro, after looking at pictures and the cameras last night, there was only one person with a red hat," he said.
I'm excited because we found him. We found the nigga that disrespected my cousin.

"Who was it" I asked.
I was ready to fuck somebody up behind my family.

"It was Ears" Dusse said.

Nah, it couldn't have been Ears. This nigga was helping us look for the dude. Now that I think about it, I told him to find the nigga with the "Red Hat". Dusse just stared at me with the most annoyed look that anyone could have.

"You had us looking for this nigga and he was right there," she said.

"I don't think he even knew we were looking for him," I said.

"He didn't" she replied.

"I spoke to him this morning and he said yea, he probably tried to bag her, but he couldn't remember," she said.

Damn, that was like Ears. Always trying to bag a girl, whether she was taken or not. After sending my cousin a picture and getting confirmation that it was Ears I feel like an idiot. Ears was a disrespectful ass nigga but never to anyone in our circle. There was clearly some type of miscommunication. We laughed about this for years to come but never told anyone the real details. We were looking for a nigga that was assisting us in his own search the entire time. I felt like an asshole, but I knew I made them look like assholes. I learned another valuable lesson that day from my own dumb actions. Following anything or anyone without proper knowledge and information is ignorance. I never played Follow the Leader again.

Stay Tuned!

You Going to Jail

All my life I was forced to go to church. My Mima and Pop made sure that we knew it wasn't an option. Even when I started living on my own, I would receive calls to wake up and get dressed. And when I didn't answer she'd just show up at my house and knock on my door.

"Randy, get yo ass up for church" she'd say.

The first missionary I knew who'd curse on the regular and would beat your ass. So, to avoid an ass whooping as a grown man, I'd get my ass up and get dressed for church. It was at church that I found out how talented I was. I could sing and play instruments, not one but multiple. And not to toot my own horn but I was good. My first passion was the drums. I started playing at the early age of 3. Just banging on the cymbals and snare but I was playing. It wasn't until I was about 13 that I started taking it seriously and became pretty awesome at it. I always knew I could sing. I was the lead singer on the little disciples. That was the name of the children's choir at the church. At home, we weren't allowed to listen to rap or R&B. Of course, we would sneak and listen to it anyway but if we got caught the consequences would be crucial. I'd listen to R. Kelly and K-ci from Jodeci and practice their runs. Trying to sneak and listen to R&B and look out for Mima was tiring though so I just stopped. I would try and find people in the gospel world who did the same thing but never could until I heard groups like the Canton Spirituals and Willie

Neal Johnson and the Keynotes. These were gospel legends in a genre of music titled Quarter Music. Quartet Music consisted of one lead singer accompanied by three background singers, singing in three-part harmony. They had a guitar player, a bass player, a keyboardist, and a drummer. When all of this came together it was angelic to my ears. What made a good quartet group was the lead singer. It was the lead singer who commanded the attention of the room with not only their singing but their charisma. They had style and charm that just made you want to listen to them. The Canton's Spiritual leader's name was Harvey Watkins Jr., and he would take songs and make them sound so close to R&B it was crazy. He would add runs in songs that you would think didn't fit. His vocal register was unbelievable and his falsetto…. UNMATCHED!

I played him so much that my grandmother thought that I would become a pastor. She was thrilled to have her young grandson so tuned to gospel music. See my Mima and Pop had a gospel group of their own. Their group consisted of them, my aunt and uncle, and two of their friends. They would call themselves Nancy and the Sons of Harmony. The name always bugged me out because my aunt was definitely in that group. So, everyone wasn't a son, she was a daughter. I later found out that she wasn't always a part of the group but was added in when they had already established an audience, so they weren't about to change the name. But the more I listened to Harvey, the more I learned. I took everything I learned and started applying it when I sang. Picture this, a young teenager singing R&B style gospel and I always dressed the part. I had all the girls and their momma's going crazy, and just like that, I was no longer singing for the lord. I was singing for the pussy. I was smashing all the women in the church. I had best friends fighting, and mothers and daughters not speaking. I was even the reason why one pastor stopped coming to our church. I smashed his First Lady real good. I started thinking though. If I could do this in the church, I'd get way more women singing R&B. Just like that I was in the studio recording my first song. I was always a lil freaky ass little boy so writing a song about it wouldn't be a problem. Exactly what I thought would happen, happened. I started getting girls from every direction. I'm just glad that I never got any diseases. Some I used condoms with and some I didn't. While I didn't catch diseases, I did catch a child. I had a beautiful daughter. 7 pounds 5 ounces, 19 inches long. She was born on February 1st at 9 pm and we would name her Love. I knew I had to change my life around. I was doing all this singing in the church and out and I was actively still in the streets. It's what the old folks would call "One foot in and one foot out". I was into everything that included trouble, but I would stop. My daughter was my first priority now, but I hated her mother. Her mother and I met in

JHS and would talk here and there but nothing serious. We did that all the way through high school and even after. The crazy thing about it is Love's mother got pregnant off pre cum. She was one of those really fake religious ppl who felt she didn't want to have sex but would still let me finger her and do almost everything else except the actual act. This one day she wanted to see what it would feel like. I was already excited, and she let me put the head in and boom. That was all it took. We wouldn't be much after that but having her as a baby mother was hell. One evening I'm at the studio and my daughter is with my mother. By this time, we've established court visitation rights and payment. It's my weekend but she decided that she wants to come and get Love. She comes over with her hood project ass family and they jump my mother and take my daughter. Why? Why is this happening? I leave the studio immediately and head to the house. Upon arrival, I saw my mother on the floor and these unstable creatures… I won't say the other word but they're standing outside. I immediately head to my room to get my gun. I walk outside and I have a clear shot but damn… Love is looking right at me. It was at that moment I decided that it wasn't worth it, but the damage was already done. They had already called the authorities and I was about to go to jail. I immediately walk off and stash my weapon. This is where I fucked up. I had the option of getting rid of my gun, but I decided to be greedy and stash it. After all, there were so many people outside how would they pinpoint me? They actually pulled up right on me. What I didn't know was that my shirt had been ripped from my mother trying to stop me from going outside. When they gave a description of me, they also included that tiny piece of information. I was in cuffs and the weapon was found in a matter of minutes. Queens back then was known for shootings, but this was my first offense. I knew I was getting 6 months of probation at max. After a couple of days of being detained, I walked into the courtroom to see everyone waiting there on my behalf. My entire family, church family, friends, and even my dad. Yeah, I had a good support system. I was definitely going home or so I thought. They set bail at

$75,000 dollars. I had money but not that much. Between what I had and then scraping up the rest I would be released through a bail bond. I had a long battle ahead of me. 2 years I went back and forth to court, fighting and arguing for my freedom. The first offer I received was 15 years. That was the first time I experienced the feeling of "My heart is in my stomach." My legs got weak, and I could barely stand. I couldn't do 15 years. I didn't even wanna do one.

"What happened to probation?" I asked my lawyer.

He explained to me that because the shooting percentages were so high in my borough they were cracking down and the time given. Wait, wait, wait….

"So, if would've had the gun in Brooklyn I would be looking at less time?" I asked. He looked at me and said,

"If you were in Brooklyn, you would've had your 6 months' probation and home already."

Now I was nervous. Anyone who says they're looking to face some real time and aren't nervous is a liar. We would do this for 2 years. My offer went from 15 years to 7 years. Then from 7yrs to 5. Ultimately, the last offer I would receive would be 3 1/2 yrs. I prepared and told myself I could do that. I started working out and mentally preparing myself for a world I had no clue about but wanted to be ready for. Then I received a call saying the judge wanted to see me. That was highly unusual. No one around me had ever heard of anything like that happening. My lawyer and I walked into the courthouse and into his chambers. He explained to me the extent of the search that he went through to research me. He had seen the gospel videos, received the letters from the community, and even spoken to multiple pastors on my behalf but the one that mattered to him the most was my lawyer's opinion. He told me that my lawyer and he were really good friends and my lawyer felt strongly about me getting the best deal possible because he felt like I was a good kid. After about 2 hours of him talking and me listening he gave me an offer that I couldn't refuse. I went home and told no one of this news. I would just enjoy my family, but I knew I had to sign these papers at my next court appearance. My family prayed and some even lied. Told me that GOD told them that I wouldn't do any time. Let's just say that GOD didn't lie, but they ass did. Fake ass prophets. I would eventually take a plea deal for 2yrs with the option of an early release through work release. Want to hear something crazy, the day I turned myself in my mother couldn't be there. She was on her way to her own court date for fraud and theft. January 19th was the start of a strenuous new era in my life. I was going to prison. Would I be a sheep or a wolf? I heard so many stories of people who enter prison with the intention of serving one amount of time but wouldn't leave at that desired time because they acquired more time. I just wanted to do my time and go home but it doesn't always work that way. I guess we'll just have to wait and see.

Stay Tuned!

About the Author

Kry Jones is a funny and outgoing entrepreneur. He spent the majority of his childhood in the church as a musician. He traveled the world ministering and encouraging others at just the early age of 11. At the age of 22, he was incarcerated on a firearm charge which eventually led to a conviction and sentence of 2 years in prison. Upon his arrival home, finding work was damn near impossible. After applying for nearly 100 jobs with no success he finally decided to take matters into his own hands. He would no longer allow his past to dictate either his present or his future. Kry established the Krown'd Kingd'm clothing line in 2017 and has been going strong ever since. In January of 2020, Kry embarked on an old passion of his and proceeded to pursue a music career. It didn't stop there, In May of 2022 he proceeded to write his first screenplay "Morals" in which he both produced and starred in. Even with all this his number one passion & priority is being both a Husband and Father. He is excited to see where this new journey will take him.